No one ever takes a photograph of something they want to forget.

Wild New Zealand

Published by

The Halcyon Press.

A division of

Halcyon Publishing Ltd.

P.O. Box 360, Auckland 1015, New Zealand.

Printed through
Colorcraft Ltd
Hong Kong

ISBN 1-877256-34-x
Copyright © 2003
All Rights Reserved

Cover photograph by:
Lance Barnard
Back cover photograph by
Tony Pidgeon
Half title page photogaph by:
Alby Frampton
Title page photograph by:
Lance Barnard

Wild New Zealand

IMAGES SELECTED BY TREVOR CHAPPELL WORDS BY DAVE BLAIR

Acknowledgements

The authors thank sincerely the following photographers for permission to use their outstanding images in this publication 'Wild New Zealand'.

Rob Suisted – www.Naturespic.com;
Lance Barnard; Tony Pidgeon;
Andy Aanensen; Richard McKenzie;
Alby Frampton; Trevor Chappell;
Paul Peychers; Andy Trowbridge;
Mark Sarjeant; Bob Ramsay;
Owen Swann; Greg Duley;
Ted Raye; Blue Thomas;
Will Rickerby; Kees Swanink;
Trevor Meikle; Chris Palffy;
Grant Morriss;
Anne C. Patterson; Mike Freeman;
Les Nelson; B. Sandford;
Geoff Wakelin; C. Murphy;
Dave Blair.

Photograph by Lance Barnard

Foreword

by Sir Paul Reeves
Governor General of New Zealand 1985-1990.

Maori, when they reached this land, used the sea and the forest as their gardens. They fished and gathered. They hunted the moa for food and they cleared land for their settlements. The later settlers from Britain were looking to create a new society of opportunity and achievement but they also saw this land as a great industrial park where the demands of the world's markets could be met with the product of the cow and the sheep.

We continue to develop our natural assets in economic terms and are tempted to put a price on everything but I sense a change. Of course we want to experience the world as fully as possible but want to leave it in good shape for those who come after us. There is a growing realisation that to own land for instance is to be trustee for succeeding generations.

A landowner with a significant piece of open space like a wetland, coastline or stand of bush is likely to take legal steps to preserve it

even if the property is subsequently sold. There are plenty of local groups who seek to restore habitat for the sake of the yellow eyed penguin, for instance, or safeguard plants that are threatened with extinction.

We are not a society that spends a lot of time and money on erecting buildings. Our monuments and the things that represent our hopes and aspirations are our mountains, our bush, our coastline and foreshore. We have great wilderness areas in New Zealand and this book contains stunning photographs of places, flora and fauna most of us will never see but form a backdrop for our lives. They are there to be enjoyed and to be protected.

Sometimes these two elements rub against each other and we are familiar with impassioned debates about access, culling overstocking and conservation. The lesson we have to learn is that sound environmental management can provide better recreational values and opportunities.

Paul Reeves

Authors' Preface

This book has been designed and written for people everywhere who treasure the natural world. It is too a celebration of all things wild, our natural country and its abundant wildlife, its rare and distinctive birds and creatures.

This wild country has retained its untamed character. The land outside of its rugged boundaries has, for the most part, been changed by man forever. But this untamed land, bushed, wild grassed, wide, tall, shaped by time and nature, changes each of us every time that we enter it.

The New Zealand Deerstalkers Association, has a vision to keep our country and its wildlife as it is, and the brief is precise; to retain the status quo in regard to New Zealand's biodiversity. I understand quite clearly the meaning of these words. But they are not the words I would personally use to express what I believe we all truly hope for, what we truly believe in. The words, in their brevity, cannot summarise all that is in our hearts and minds, all that is precious to us. It is not just the animals we seek to protect; it is the total environment. These brief words give no value to beauty, to the sheer magnificence of this singularly astonishing gathering of islands, the nature if which is found nowhere else on earth. What we have is the envy of the world. Land that climbs, runs, tumbles, slides, rolls in endless hills, falls into fjords, stacks itself, bushed hill upon hill to peaks sharp, sheer, jagged, hung with snow against skies of the sharpest blue. No words are adequate to truly describe its splendour, its birds and insects, its bountiful wildlife.

So here we have assembled, not only for those New Zealanders to whom natural beauty and wildlife are a treasure, but also for those who visit our shores with too little time to see such sights, a superb collection of photographs. Through the enterprise of creating this volume we hope to drive the cause of keeping this nation's land, birds and animals as time, man and history have so far evolved them; whether by wisdom, foolishness, or accident, to be not only as they are, but as the majority of New Zealanders wish them to remain to be, as time and the elements continue to change not only the land, but we who treasure it.

*The fallow are well
established throughout
New Zealand from
Northland to the deep
south. In many places
they survive in small
patches of bush near
farmland, or in warm
pine forests, but they
are found too, in some
harsh country. That we
should all be free to
watch or to hunt for
them is a right we
should treasure, for they
were once, not so long
ago in the fact of time,
reserved only for kings.
May their future history
record, not only their
survival, but also the
continuance of that
kingly right.*

Lake Taupo, New Zealand's biggest lake, is the water filled crater of a great explosion and the centrepiece of the high central plateau. Within sight of its waters lie mountains, farmland, bushland, scrub-covered pumice, a desert.

The wild goats

*Like cheeky children, the goats of the
bush and hills are remembered best for
games played out on rocky bluffs, fallen
trees, and riverbeds. Comical, and with
little fear of man the goats can make
your worst days end a pleasure, as you
watch their twilight games.*

*The kids imitate every move the adults
make, emphasising the sheer joy of
living that they project in their wild
dances. They run, turn in the air, dance,
then pretend to fight fiercely but with
poor success, for their nodding butts are
too weak to be convincing. They stand
on their hind legs, balancing, then move
a few vertical steps as if comically
imitating man, then run at each other.
They stop only at the last moment to
turn and race around their rocky home,
wide-eyed, tails pointing to the sky, their
long ears flapping like tassels on a
dancer. If life was meant to be fun the
goats surely know it.*

Rivers

A river, a shallow braid of rippling sound that mixes

with the rush of the wind in the beech trees, like music.

Photographs by Andy Aanensen

Left: Wild goat by M Sarjeant

Right: Kaka by Andy Aanensen

We can only imagine if the deer ran into the strange new plants to hide, or perhaps pause to look for what they knew and remembered. A hump of rising ground, a hollow where a trickling beck might lead them to safety, hidden from the sight of man as they had known him; cloth cap, tweed trousers, tall hunting boots, crommach in his hand, his ghillie close behind with the rifle... How the red deer ran we will never know now, for those who saw them step out from their barred crate that day are long gone, so no witness survives to relate the tale.

Right: Spiker by Lance
Barnard

Far right: Flight by
Trevor Chappell

This look of innocence will go. The spiker will soon learn that in the bush, to fear is to survive.
The lessons of life in the wild have begun, to look, to listen, to run. The deer is a flight animal whose eyes and
ears tell them when to run, when to hide; for speed is their only weapon.

The frog

Green, silent, still and shining, the green frog patiently waits for a fly to pass by his magic eye. Fly or insect he shows them quick, death in the lightning lash of his tongue.

Photograph by Richard McKenzie

Left: Mountain stream by Trevor Chappell

North Island bush by Trevor Chappell

Ruru the owl

His wide-eyed wise look hides the heart of a hunter; his mournful call a warning. When night comes, the eyes of ruru see all. On his quiet wings he becomes the silent knight of death, unseen, swift, sure and unerring.

Photograph by Andy Trowbridge

The kea

With a rainbow under his wings and mischief in his eyes, the kea is the wild country vandal. A wrecker of camps, and the mountains cheerful clown.

Photograph by Richard McKenzie

The opossum

I remember him, red-eyed and innocent in the torch's beam, hacking like a hardened smoker in the black night. We hear him scratching on the hut's tin roof in winter, see him scampering through spring grass at its end. He is called Jacko, possum, coon, this stealer of apples, thief of time, national pest. The dogs may often be on his tail and a bounty on his head, but paradoxically he may end his life more honoured than most, as a fur coat, or the most expensive jersey in the tourist shop.

Photograph by Andy Trowbridge

The blue heron

They stalk graceful and shy on the edge of water where they are most often seen. Their flight is ponderous and unstable and they seem always to be unsure of their navigation. Their subtle colours of grey and blue touched with white are striking and somehow appear to suit their solitary anti-social ways.

Photograph by Owen Swann

Ducks by Dave Blair

Emerald Lakes by C. Murphy

Right: Red deer roaring by Tony Pidgeon

Far right: Golden Valley by Will Rickerby

Wild horses

As has been their fate in other countries, our wild horses have alternately been hunted, preserved, mustered, auctioned, farmed, then broken to the ways of man.

I saw my first wild horse as an eighteen-year-old soldier at Waiouru in the central North Island. My first view of the horses was from a gold tussocked hill that looked down on a river. The place was named Paradise Valley, and at dawn with the first light of the sun on their fat shiny bodies as they splashed into the river led by a black stallion, and a few sika deer ran off, frightened by their wild approach, the valley seemed well named.

Where fog lingered in the valley and patches of beech forest climbed up the hillsides, the tussock rippled in the first faint breeze, turning and swaying at the whim of the wind, the soft light dancing off it. Out to the east, distant wild hills scarred with slips lay pink in the dawn. I did not know then how the horses had come to be there, only that they were, and it was a grand sight to see them. I could not foresee then, their muddled insecure future, the helicopters that would in time come to drive them in fear across that wild country.

I worked with horses then, one of the last to do so in the farming way, following behind the plough, the mower, the hayrake and the harrows, singing out the remembered commands of my grandfather, the blacksmith, the farmer.

I looked for the one I could imagine under me, thundering over that wild untamed country. The big black stallion ruled the herd, magnificent, glossy coated, he bullied the mares and the young ones out of the river, nodding his head, saying in the language of the horse, go, or I will make you go. I knew his language, so too did his herd. Soon they were cresting the ridge above the river silhouetted against the rising sun. 'Get down soldier, there's an airstrike coming in!' I was pulled back out of my dream, back into the world of soldier games. Nothing so fiercely breaks the wilderness' peace quite like the voice of man. Just then I preferred the company of the horses, and the wild, wild land they live in. Photograph by Dave Blair

The sika deer

Most beautiful of all the deer is the sika, their only challenger the elegant Virginian whitetail. To watch them move in their hesitant gait is a magical thing. The sika is the favourite of many. Their curiosity is an endearing characteristic, yet it is too often the cause of their premature demise.

They are curious, yet elusive, the eye that watches you from behind a tree, the slice of red body seen between the trunks of the tall forest beech, always only shows a piece of the animal, like putting together a puzzle.

A sika stag in his summer coat has no rival as the most striking animal you will find in the forest and scrublands where he is found. The beech forests east of Taupo are beautiful places in themselves, though the sika seem to prefer to live in the thick fringing manuka scrub if given the opportunity, just as the red deer will run to the bush if left to decide between bush or scrublands. In the scrublands the sika seems to feel safer, and it is warm there when the cold mountain winds blow, and too when the winter snows come blustering across the land, transforming it into a ghostly magical world.

The sika whistles at your approach all year, so the forest is never completely quiet. But when the chill winds of April blow and the stags are stirred in their rut, there comes a new excitement to the forest. Every sound from the mewing of a cat to the scream of an angry bull comes out of the sika stag. He is a vocal wizard who can just as adeptly stalk the hunter, as the hunter stalks him. All of his troubles come from the innate curiosity that he is born with and seems unable to control, in spite of the danger that it brings to him.

Everything about these animals draws us, the land that they live in, their captivating elegance, their curiosity. It is not only the sight of the rutting stag we remember, but that of the females, with their big oval eyes, that glorious spotted summer coat, their pointed noses, their alert ears that are never still, and with them, mirrored in nature, April fawns, tiny images of their mothers. Their wild country is a powerful magnet to us, the rolling scrublands patched with pockets of deep green beech. The forest itself with its open glades, its dense tight valleys of horipito, its great faces of ferns that cover the slopes like combed hair, the rattling heads of the scattered cabbage trees. Life there would not be the same without the sounds of the birds who follow the deer, so we know when to be alert for animals, and when to relax and stroll through the country as if we are taking a walk in a park.

Photograph by Bob Ramsay

A meandering river winds through tussock flats, bordered by thick manuka scrub that leads through leaping terraces to the peaceful beech forest. This is the home of the sika and the red deer, the possum and the night owl, and the birds of the day, the tui and the bush robin and the pigeon, the wildlife that lives in the often misty rain-soaked world of the Kaimanawa and Kaweka Mountains. Autumn brings new sounds to the country, the roar of the red stag and the whistles and screams of the sika. The land seems transformed then, as if the country has suddenly changed from black and white, to colour

Far Left: Mt Ngauruhoe by Trevor Chappell
Right: Oamaru River valley by Trevor Chappell

Left: Rushing water by Trevor
   Chappell

Below Fungi by
Trevor Chappell

The wild sow

With an intellect as sharp as her napoleonic nose, a sow patiently waits and listens in silence. As the clever pig does, she will not panic, but think before she moves. Caught out among the summer flowering ragwort she stands out sharply black against her colourful backdrop of gold and green.

Photograph by Trevor Chappell

Bush fungi

The damp bush produces a
kaleidoscope of coloured
fungi. Orange, blue, brown,
white, red and green. They
sit sometimes in a bed of
moss, or simply spring up
among the roots of a giant
tree, as if sheltering there.
Sometimes they stand like
policemen, a huddle of blue
helmets, others as a show of
bright red umbrellas, like
something out of a child's
fairyland dream.

Photograph by Trevor Chappell

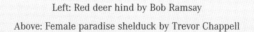

Left: Red deer hind by Bob Ramsay
Above: Female paradise shelduck by Trevor Chappell

Left: Possum by
Trevor Chappell

Below: Fungi by
Trevor Chappell

Wild merinos

*These tough and ragged
sheep are descendants of
rogue sheep who long ago
were clever enough to
escape shepherd and dog to
gain the freedom of high
tussock and warm bush.
Caught in the open they
appear as vagrant tramps,
always bedraggled, looking
as if the whole world is
against them.*

Photograph by Trevor Chappell

The tomtit is small but cheerful company to the lone traveller, a bright spark of life on a bleak day.

Photograph by Mark Sarjeant

Waterfalls

To the beauty of a waterfall
nature adds its hollow sound of
endlessly falling water that
changes its song with the seasons.
A soft trembling echo through a
long dry summer, a roaring
torrent in a winter storm; the
moods of life in water.

Photograph by Andy Aanensen
Right: Looking back by Bob Ramsay

Above: Wild pig by Trevor Chappell

Right: Fallow buck by Rob Suisted

The fantail

A sure sign of winter, the aerobatic fantail in a bare tree.

Photograph by Trevor Chappell

Until the autumn's rut the fallow are quiet deer. Their only sounds of flight a sudden flurry of hooves, the huge white flare of their tails showing as clear as a bushman's new blaze mark on a tree.
The fallow's vocal opposite, the sika is almost always first heard, then seen. Their warning whistle seems to follow you for a while, as if they are calling you back.

Left: Fallow deer by
Trevor Chappell

Right: Sika deer by
Bob Ramsay

The rivers

They are born in the land yet destined for the sea; that boundless sea that touches all the world. There they are reborn into clouds to come home again, as rain, or crystals to tip a mountain white.

Photograph by Mark Sarjeant

Old or new there is nothing like the sight of a hut in the hills, looming out of the gloom on a miserable day. The old ones remain the most endeared, like old bush characters. The water drum, the smoking chimney, wood stacked against a rusty wall. Who cares if the roof leaks a little, inside it's warm and full of history and stories.

Hut by Trevor Chappell

Right: Sika by Greg Duley

The Indian sambar

He could be made of bronze so clear is his silhouette upon the dawn sky. He seems unaware of his outline on the sandhill ridge among the lupins. This is how I find him each morning as I ride out to shepherd my block of the station's sheep. There are 1600 sheep grazing this piece of country that stretches from pine tree plantation acres to lupin-studded paddocks of ewes and lambs. On the edge of the farmland the country turns wild, running to low sandhills covered by flaxes, broom, lupins and patches of manuka scrub, gorse and sand-grasses. This is the home of the sambar, though you would not know it were your eyes not sharp to their sign, or you slept late. The sambar is a deer of the night, a nocturnal mystery.

Like their cousins the rusa deer, they are furtive. In captivity they are constantly trying to hide themselves, and it seems cruel to keep them with no place to hide, for daylight has always been their enemy. Instilled in their genes is their desire for darkness. If there is only one small lonely shrub, they will all be found trying to hide behind it.

If you disturb him during the day the sambar will not run until, like a startled pheasant, you are on top of him. Then, he leaps from the bed where he has lain, his antlers pinned to his back, his neck outstretched, all of him as flat on the face of the earth as he can make himself. He looks a little foolish to me, because I am mounted on my high horse and can clearly see him lying there. Once he is up and running he will stop for nothing. He runs as the females do, though to a lesser extent, in a half crouch, his head at knee-height like a scenting spaniel. The sambar slip through fences where they have stretched the wires over the many times they have travelled there, or leap quickly and elegantly over, not seeming to alter their crouch, like burglars.

The sambar seems to have a broad breeding season so you may see a hard antlered stag and one still in velvet on the same day. The hunting season is set for September and October so most sambar stags seem to be in hard antler by spring.

Second only to the wapiti as the largest of the deer, their meat is coarse and dark and not particularly favoured as venison. Other than man the sambar has no enemies. Our farm dogs though would chase them without any encouragement, if we let them.

Photograph by Rob Suisted

The sambar's hearing is exceptional, as you would expect of an animal of the night, and his big bat ears are constantly on the move, so he hears one moment behind him, the next to one side, then listening to where he travels, ahead. Like his cousin the rusa, his huge ears are his means to survival, his daylight burglar alarm, his night-time radar.

Sambar family by Trevor Chappell

Right: Coastal country by Richard McKenzie

The Californian quail

Strutting plume-headed like some Russian Hussar, the little quail cock presents an arrogant figure as he bravely shepherds his flock. In their striking blue-grey colours, their flecked chests and that distinctive upright crest, the quail have all the pomp and bearing of soldiers on parade.

Their survival ploy is simple – speedy flight that is familiar to all that travel their domain of scrublands, crop, or country field of waving grain. If they choose to, quail can run at an astonishing speed. Eventually though it is always flight that takes them from us, their wingbeats rapid whipsaw hum as familiar as their cheery crow.

The bush pigeon

Once the favourite food of
the Maori the bush pigeon
is now protected. The loud
rush of wings that
announce his arrival often
startles the bush traveller
whose company they seem
to seek.

Photograph by Paul Peychers

The seal

A sea dweller, the seal is angry, noisy, clumsy, footless and irritated as he lies on the tide lashed rocks of the shore. Yet put him in his home the sea and he becomes an aquatic missile, as sleek, smooth and graceful as any creature born there.

Photograph by Richard McKenzie

Red deer

It can be said only of the red deer, that no other New Zealand animal has been liberated into such a diverse variety of landscapes, from the north to the south of this elongated land of ours. Wherever we have placed them they have been surrounded by wild beauty. Whether in the lowland forests, the high South Island tops, or the deep rain-drenched valleys of Fiordland. Each of these inspiring places has their own particular beauty. The lowlands whose bushclad, high grassed, bare patched ridges lie at interrupted angles, are divided and watered by stony, clear, unpolluted streams such as are found nowhere else on earth. Grassy clearings line their streams, and at the very height of the bushed land, one can look out across the tumbling mass, its tops tan coloured above faces and valleys textured in a thousand greens that run humped and tumbled into distance.

Photograph by
Geoff Wakelin

Canada goose

You cannot mistake their raucous honking voices, whether they come softly from across a misty lake or are more

The pheasant

The country recluse, his crow is a welcome sound on bleak winter mornings. His shape is a bright jewel in those short dark days, a welcome splash of colour at the coming of summer.

On a misty morning a flurry of wing-beats lifts him into a long glide over the ragged rolling land he lives in. He falls into the tall grass, runs, goose steps, and crows again. He lifts your spirits with his sound, and always without fail, he captures our hearts with his show of the true and simple freedom of wild places.

Photograph by Grant Morriss

Arapawa sheep

They come from an older time, from a cold and

bleak place where only the hardy survive.

Photograph by Kees Swanink

Left: Evening over water by Richard McKenzie

The falcon

The elegance and grace that typify the falcon's flight become lost on the ground. There he is clumsy and ungainly. But this bold bird's vigilant eyes are unchanging, tack sharp and fearless, he observes the wild land from on high, wheeling in great circles, forever the hunter, a piece of nature's art on the wing; his flight always smooth as a windless pond.

Photograph by Paul Peychers

Right: Fallow doe by Paul Peychers

The tui

The handsomest bird to be found in the bushland, the tui's voice is the most musical in the forest. The bellbird imitates him, yet the song, unmistakable, is the tui's alone.

Photograph by Owen Swann

Scene left: Okuru River By Ted Raye

When we look down on the land from on high in an aircraft it is easy to recall the words of the Danish
writer Karen Blixen who saw such a view of the world from one of the first aircraft to fly in Africa.
' The greatest gift of all; a glimpse of the world through God's eyes.'

Photograph by Tony Pidgeon

High country

When we talk of high country, I think of the country east of the Southern Alps. In recollection of it I see many things. There are shepherds, dogs, nailed boots by the back door, merinos pouring in a grey flood over hill and valley, the individual sheep blended into a solid moving frayed-edged mass, that, seething with the energy of swarming bees breaks this way and that, unpredictable as the weather. High country is early starts, barking dogs, hot porridge, woollen hats, hill sticks, a gas lamp hissing in a quiet hut, the fire roaring inside, the wood stacked high outside. High country is pack horses, mist filled valleys, tussock, matagouri, briars, yellow tracked hills, boiling billies, red sunsets, mutton stew, mountains, snow, rain, sun, sleet, showers falling in grey curtains across

the hills. The peace of a waking valley when the hills are cleared, the clinking shoes of the horses in the riverbed, a stag roaring, chamois dancing high in the pink dawn.

High country is people's troubles shared, a thin creek, a fat river, the year of the drought, the big flood, the time it snowed early and the sheep were trapped high for a week. Hay fed in the cold spring, a thin gold line of grain, the following sheep, waving wheat, the first faint bleat of a lamb.

At day's end the sight of the homestead paddocks, hand shears clicking, the ring of laughter, a hut full of stories. The moonlight on a sparkling frost, a kea's cry, a fat cheque, a sad goodbye; gratitude at being chosen to see it all, to be there, in the high country.

Photographs, left by
Ted Raye, above by
Richard McKenzie

Many an adventurer into this wild landscape has topped a ridge to find no recognisable landmark before him, for each ridge seems a cloned brother of the last. Compass-less, the journey before him assumes nightmare proportions. Even with the guiding needle in his hand a hard slog across the endless lines of hills lies before the traveller. No easy road is to be found for the compass has no versatility; knows only one unerring route, always it seems across the rise and fall of the land.

Photograph by Tony Pidgeon
Right: Photograph by Chris Palffy

Right: This stag could be standing in the Scottish Highlands wild summer grass, not South Island tussock. He would be at home in either country, for wherever there are vast desolate open mountains, there you will find him, elegant and alert, one bound away from his frantic run to freedom.

Photograph by Trevor Meikle

Above: George Sound by Paul Peychers

The pancake rocks of
Punakaiki have been eaten
away, land and stone, into
strange and haunting
shapes by the restless West
Coast seas. They stand like
man made statues with the
green waves always beating
at their feet. The beach
sands are as black and
forbidding as the rough wet
country at whose edge they
lie, and the beaches are
littered with the shapes of
giant tree roots, like
wreckage. Occasionally we
find the bright shape of a
trawler's lost buoy; bright
orange against the black of
the sand.

Photograph by Les Nelson

West Coast beach by B Sandford

Storm sky by Paul Peychers

In velvet the red stag changes. He is often hidden now for he must protect his new growing armour until it hardens ready for the autumn battles for the right to a herd of hinds. In twelve weeks he will have grown as much as twelve kilos of bone tissue from nothing, as fast as the growth of any tumour. Then as if by magic, the growth stops and hardens. The velvet antler has long been held to be a wonder medicine in Asia. It is better known here now for its properties as an aphrodisiac, and is widely recognised for its benefits in the treatment of both arthritis and Parkinson's disease and to enhance the performance of athletes.

Photograph by Mike Freeman

To look across this landscape of peak and cloud and valley conjures visions an impossible journey for all but the hardiest traveller. But it is not impossible; few things are to the willing mind.

Photograph by Alby Frampton

A true white fallow buck as fine as this is a rare sight. Stark as marble against the forest's darkness he appears so ghost-like you might wonder that if you looked away, then found him gone, that he was ever there at all.

Photograph by Paul Peychers

Our wild hills have an extraordinary power to lure us time and again into their midst. No bad memory of wild winds or rain, nor sleet or snowstorm remains strong enough in the minds of the people of the hills and mountains to deter their returning to the wild places. It is in fact our vivid memories of the bad days that challenge us to return. A few words spoken of their magic and the memories come back, and plans for new adventures rise up in us. Soon forgotten are the hard days, boots heavy in the snow, cold chilling us to our very hearts. Disappointment at our failure to climb a peak, or find an animal that dissolves into land with no obvious place to hide, clouds our minds, blinding us to the beauty that surrounds us, and our very reason for being there. Soonest remembered by the traveller, the sight of the sun climbing out of the misty hills, the river sparkling below us, a twinkling jewel in the mountain valley. We remember easily the way the country unravels before us as we travel, the miles marked by hours, the days by dates, for the name of the day has no relevance for the man on the hill. The people of the wild country, once free in the wilderness the hills and mountains, need no time signal to begin their day or to end it. Our clock is the light that paints the land in changing colours, until black, grey, or the silver of moonlight, leads us to a temporary home, be it hut or tent, a cave, a dry rock or a sheet of polythene. Gone for the time of our stay, the electric stove, the toaster, kettles, showers or powerbills, for the places we seek, while we are there are ours alone. The world is about us, the real world, earth, stone, tree and sky. Freedom is our right, energy our money, the grass that whispers in the wind, the rattling creek, the distant roaring stag, our entertainment. Our day done the animals fall silent as we do, and only the creek sings its endless song to the night.

Photograph by Anne C. Patterson

Were it not for the scale of the tiny human figure one could not for a moment grasp the immensity of this ice-bound landscape. Like the glacier opposite this land is always changing, a living thing ever growing and shrinking with the passing of time. Time that is both ally and enemy; master of all things, and of humanity itself.

Photograph by Trevor Chappell

Far left: At the foot of the glacier by Tony Pidgeon

The Himalayan tahr

I am the mountains' king,
Master of the ice;
Ruler of the snows.

He is the undisputed king of the mountains, and probably the most highly prized of all of the animals. His home is the highest, the most dangerous to visit. It is a place for mountaineers, and the tahr is the mountaineer par excellance, the Edmund Hillary of the animals.

You cannot mistake what he is when you find him where he belongs, in this place where few can follow. The icy wind will have picked up his silver-white mane from behind and driven it around the sweep of his horns. This is how he stands, his black rump to the wind, his slim pointed muzzle thrust forward as he gazes out from a high shelf that gives him a fine view of his mountain world. The high snow-clad peaks surround him; grey jagged stone falls away below his perch. Coloured shale slides divide the sharp ridges where the thin short cropped tussock that sustains him, holds together his fragile world.

His herd stands above and about him, the nannies forever alert to danger. One sharp muffled whistle and they will all be gone. Their descent off the mountain is magical, daring and courageous. They fall, tumble in the snow, come up out of it like skiers from powdered snow, and run again, never appearing to look back at the source of their danger until they feel they are safe.

The tahr have in their time been harried, hunted, slaughtered in their thousands and left to decay on the cold slopes of their high home. They have been protected by one government decree, destroyed by another, yet revered always and only by the people of the hills and the lovers of wild animals, as a unique and majestic creature with an astonishing ability to breed and survive where most would perish.

It is the tahr who has been held accountable for the destruction of mountain vegetation; in particular the Mount Cook lily. But of those who name the tahr the villain, none can say that after more then a hundred years of sharing the same mountains, that the lily has gone and only the tahr remain.

Photograph by Tony Pidgeon

In the shadow of the mountain.

Chamois

Photograph by Tony Pidgeon

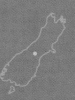

The Austrian chamois

I am the clown,
The mountain my circus arena.
It costs nothing to laugh at my foolishness,
All mountain shows are free.

Surely the most graceful of our mountain animals, the chamois have a charm all of their own. Acrobatically elusive, they dance their way through the mountains with a natural skill.

The chamois has the seeming ability to move his body in three different directions at once, yet still he moves predominantly forward with sufficient speed to take him swiftly to safety. The chamois can be difficult animals to follow. Even though they live far below the lofty heights of their fellow mountaineers, the Himalayan tahr, they have the ability to climb into extremely steep country. Theirs is the world of deep snow tussock, the spiked Spaniards and matagouri scrub on stony faces, and the alpine plants whose ability to survive the harsh mountain climate is well matched by the chamois.

A big buck is a magnificent animal. Powerfully formed, with a deep chest and muscled rump, he runs at a speed that belies his stocky build. The chamois is difficult to keep in captivity and will kill any other antelope put near them. Their horns are the sharpest of all our animals, as many have discovered.

To see the chamois at play, at dusk, or in the silver early morning light, is to watch an animal ballet. Their twisting, turning, bouncing antics take them in and out of rocky gullies with mercurial speed. They turn in mid-air as if equipped with unseen wings, their bodies twisted, their heads turned back, as if to admire their own frantic flight. The display is all too brief, for soon they move out onto the grass and drift through the scrub to graze, well camouflaged in their uniform of shades that imitate the colours of the country they belong to. The fawns and blacks and browns, dark and light, blend into the land, so the chamois seems to disappear and reappear as if by some mountain trick of magic.

Photograph by Tony Pidgeon

It is sad to think that politics has for so long sought to destroy them. One would think that it would not be too difficult to find places for them where they would not conflict with other animals or humanity; yet history shows this not to be true. The Austrian chamois is I think, here to stay; only the place and size of his home is in doubt. In truth, if we wish it to be, a place can be found for all of our animals. All that is required is willingness on the part of mankind for any grand plan to transpire.

Left: Photograph by Andy Trowbridge
Right: Photograph by Lance Barnard

The chamois

They are the acrobats of the mountains who can turn in the sky as if it were possible to grip the air. At dusk they catch the eye with their sharp black silhouettes dancing on the colours of the shale.

Source of a river

The higher we climb the steepening river, the purer the water that hurries through her time-worn stones. At our feet grow tussock and mountain flowers. Ahead, mountain mist sits in the valley beyond stunted high-level beech trees that, hardened by time and the wind, are bent to the mountains' shape. This is country so truly wild that it will through the centuries remain so, like an animal that cannot be tamed.

Photograph by Tony Pidgeon
Right: Young tahr by Tony Pidgeon

*To the tahr, no
mountaineering feat seems
impossible. On near vertical
faces of stone they cling as
close as the moss and lichens
they feed on. Bodies of
animals are often found at
the foot of steep slopes, so we
know that the tahr, for all
their fearless versatility, are
not infallible.*

Photographs by Tony Pidgeon

The wild pig

All animals have some predominant asset that sets them apart from others. The pig's is his shining intelligence. Sadly his cleverness cannot save him from the dogs he is most often persued by. Without the aid of dogs those who chase the pig would come a poor second to the pig's bright mind. Soon the pig would rule the forest by sheer numbers for they are grand survivors.

In New Zealand the pig is the most likely animal to harm you if given the chance. He is well armed and capable of inflicting severe injury to the careless, particularly if you enter the pig's domain in the bracken fern tunnels where there are no passing lanes where pig and man may separate. One quick turn of his powerful head and his tusks will have ripped your calf muscle from your leg and the pig will be gone, leaving you hurt and bleeding in the fern.

Right: Photograph by
Andy Trowbridge
Far right: Photograph
by Trevor Meikle

The mighty stag may have the finest armaments, but few animals other than the pig or the spirited sika have been known to use their weapons against man in the wild. The pig of course wants only to defend himself, his anger only aroused by the actions of man or dog. To hunt the pig without dogs is a hard task, especially a boar.

Wild pigs love the pine forests. There are warm places to make their beds of pine needles and grasses and the many plants that make up the thick undergrowth. There is protection too among the thick knotted vines of the blackberries, and where the trees are younger, the sharp spined gorse.

In the heat of summer the pines smell sweet, and the gorse when it is in flower colours gold the land among the green pines and fills the air with its thick sweet scent.

There is often a distinct lack of birdlife where there are pigs, quite the opposite of the situation where there are deer, when one might just as well go home if the birds are gone.

Of course there are places where birds, deer and the pigs live quite happily together, though it is always the pigs who are first to be pushed out by any disturbance, or simply as they inevitably do in their nomadic way, move on. The pigs are prolific breeders, and where the country is good to them they always seem to come back, as if in their great intelligence they have discovered the secret of eternal life.

Red deer

The only truly pure red deer among those that were brought here came from the Highlands of Scotland. From Blackmount Forest, and Glenavon, and from Invermark. They were true Highland deer who had known before their sea travel only the lonely barren glens and burns of a land as harsh as any in Europe. This land they had been brought so far to make their home in was harsh too, but here there was food aplenty, and the same freedom of the mountains they had known all of their short lives.

What thoughts might have crossed their minds as they stepped warily out of their shipping crate home onto soft giving grass that ran to scrub-fringed bushland. High above them and unseen yet, lay seas of waving windswept snowgrass, stone-strewn above green sawtooth fingers of bush that speared steeply upward into the golden high country grass.

We might think for them to run to the bush, as the deer would now. But there had been nowhere to hide in the Scottish Highland forestlands; for forestland had long been a misnomer in the glens. The forests had long gone, only the name remained. The land there was stony, weak grassed, the highest of its growth the odd lonely stunted tree. The rest of it, where not roughed with bracken fern, lay heather covered, purple in the last of summer, browning in the autumn under the first frosts. Among all this, mossy stoned ground, rambling, and all of it mist shrouded, gloomy, hard as flint, cold as an artic night.

Photograph by Andy Trowbridge

In time the classic Scottish head was to be perfectly portrayed by the English artist Edwin Landseer in his famous painting- 'The Monarch of the Glen.' The stag stands as if he is truly before you, so lifelike as to be real. He has come up on to the crest of a mountain and stands bold upon the Highlands, clear- eyed, alert to all about him. His head is up as if he hears yet cannot yet see who dares to enter upon his mountain. Beyond him, fresh in my mind as I have just seen them lurk dark wild hills gathered in storms, like a huddle of grumbling old men, seething with the discontents of old age, contemplating death with maliced eye, and jaundiced tongue.

Photographs by Lance Barnard

Whio the blue duck

Whio is as much a part of the wilderness as any tree or stone. Their plumage reflects the colours of the world they belong to, the gunmetal grey of mountain faces, the blue of the wide sky, the bright silver shine of fast water. Even their calls echo the bush life in the sounds of the rubbing branches of the beech trees.

Photograph by Paul Peychers

Right: Misty waterfall by Owen Swann

The hare

No other animal so amplifies the loneliness of open wild country. Perhaps it is his diminutive size that presents him as so brave a figure, so infinitesimal a creature in the great emptiness of the open wild grass, the stony wide riverbeds, the tumbling brown tussocked hills. The hare is a nomad, only a curling fringe of tussock roofs him from the elements. He is the high country tramp, living hard, asking little of the world.

Photograph by Andy Trowbridge

The wallaby
A native of Australia, the wallaby are now found north to south from Kauwau Island through Rotorua to Waimate and on. At night, caught in a beam of light they stand out like motionless eared letterboxes, a curious sight before they bound away into the gloom.
Photograph by Kees Swanink

This is a land too of storms, and a Fiordland storm is surely an unforgettable thing. Rumbling black clouds seethe in fury over the mountains to overtake all, the peaks, the bush, the rivers, the still dark lakes, the wapiti and the red deer, the birds and man. When it rains you stand, as if in a stinging shower so powerful is its weight. All of the mountain faces become waterfalls that are hurled back up into the sky by the power of the storms carrying wind. Lightning illuminates the land in all its detail and thunder reverberates through every deep bushed valley, lingering long after the storm has passed in the minds of those who witness it.

A Fiordland storm is a memory for life, and after it is over, to those lucky enough to hear them echo from on high, come those haunting bugles of the wapiti that reach out of the mountains as if from heaven itself.

Photograph by Tony Pidgeon

The fallow deer

Of all the animals introduced to our shores none better represents the true England from which they came than the proud fallow. At some time almost every great house of England have held, or still do hold, fallow in their private parklands. Their meat has become highly prized for it is fine texture and full of the flavours of the forest. In the park forests the fallow have always been jealously protected by gamekeepers who were, and perhaps still are, for the most part, retired, or at least reformed poachers, better paid to protect than left to poach.

The fallows' antlers too are greatly prized, for since the demise of the gigantic Irish elk, they remain the only animals with palmed antlers, other than the Scandinavian moose, to survive in Europe. Still today they remain the park favourites, impossible not to be noticed with their elegant shapes and their graceful movement.

Photographs by Lance Barnard

The Fiordland wapiti

As with all of our other deer species the wapiti have been alternately, protected, slaughtered, fought over, seen the making of fortunes, the loss of others. They have been captured for profit, threatened with extinction, and all the while too, revered by all who truly know them.

A big wapiti bull's steps are hesitant, syncopated. Rather than walk he seems to stalk his way along. He is known to us by the name the American Indians gave him, wapiti, white deer, though many are more yellow than white. A bull is taller than a man to the top of his head, and he is almost three metres long nose to tail. His antlers can grow to more than 60 inches; even then they look small above his huge body. To see him wild in the rut is a magical thing, the way his breath condenses in the cold morning air, billowing out of him in great clouds. His white sides heave, his head is held up, his sharp nose pointing heavenwards. The sound of his bugle lingers in the still air, sometimes as clear as the notes of an organ, at others like a frightening rasping scream that fills all the valley with its power.

To hear his magical call in the wild is to be stirred heart and soul by it, as all that hear him are. In the midst of the massive country we have placed him in, he stands equal to its magnificence. His call is a bugled voluntaire to the animals, to the hills and mountains, a melodic song of the wilderness that echoes his, and the lands, powerful hold on all who know it.

In New Zealand we have placed the wapiti in the most astonishing, the most awe inspiring and difficult country in the world. Fiordland is a place of curved valleys of bush-land beneath soaring snow-crested stone mountains; her mist filled valleys steaming in a perpetual shining wetness. The country runs west from Lake Te Anau's many jutting arms that spear in dark fingers into Fiordland's mountainous heart. It runs then through the jumbled tumbling mass of her mountains' lakes and valleys to the rugged West Coast and, where there she falls as if exhausted into deep dark fjords, then into the quiet sea.

Photograph by Paul Peychers

*Mountain and glacier, snow
and ice, a symphony in blue
and white. Beauty
unsurpassed, breathtaking
when you are there,
magnificent here on the
page as we sit warm and
removed in a room, safe
from the dangers of their
perilous slopes.*

Photographs by Tony Pidgeon

The jewelled gecko is a creature from the hidden world of wildlife that surrounds us wherever we travel in wild country. You may not often see them, but they are always about us, in bush or bog, by river or stream. The skinks are most often fleetingly seen, for they are the lizards of the day, fast and alert. The gecko is mainly a creature of the night, and slow to move. Perhaps his lack of speed accounts for his small family of two live young when the skink seldom has less the five.

Photographs by
Andy Trowbridge
Far left: Mountain bush by
Alby Frampton

Above and left:
Whitetail deer by
Blue Thomas

The whitetail deer

    The deer thrived on Stewart Island, bred too well perhaps for their antlers never reached any great size. The whitetail never lacked for food, so perhaps it was the wrong food, or there was no great fertility in that wild island's soil. They have often been found feeding on seaweed on the island's beaches, though the calcium they need to grow fine antlers probably wasn't present in that food of the sea.

    Stewart Island was always a wild place, and probably always will be. It is a lumpy land of unreliable winds, thick undergrowth and difficult access. When I hear myself describe the land I think it sounds too difficult to travel in. In truth it is said to be a grand challenge and no doubt worth the effort to see the new era of deer that now inhabit that tough little land. The deer are thinned down and now bucks can be found there with finer antlers than have been seen for many years.

    Stewart Island is now our newest National Park. How this will ultimately affect the animals that inhabit this wild most southern land of ours remains to be seen. If given voices we all know what the park's whitetail deer would say. "You gave us a home, why would you take it away?"

The kakapo

Their tubby humorous figures make them one of Fiordland's finest characters. Their close-clipped, pellet-strewn trails through the high snowgrass advertise their presence as loud as a fanfare of trumpets. It would be a great loss to the nation if they were to fail to survive, but it is certain that their chances of survival are at best, precarious.

The kiwi

We have taken his Maori name as our own; named our sports teams in their honour. The original image of the kiwi stamps ten thousand things this land produces, and sets us apart from the world in all we do. Sadly this proud national treasure diminishes in numbers as the years progress, and they are found nowhere else in the world. Only the power of money and the words of politicians can save them.

Photographs by Rob Suisted

We give the last word to The American Indian Chief Seattle

Care for the animals,

for without them

man will die from a loneliness of the spirit.